This

Bible Story Time

book belongs to

_____

For Lucy - E.C.

Text by Sophie Piper
Illustrations copyright © 2005 Estelle Corke
This edition copyright © 2005 Lion Hudson

The moral rights of the author and illustrator
have been asserted

A Lion Children's Book
an imprint of
Lion Hudson plc
Wilkinson House, Jordan Hill Road,
Oxford OX2 8DR, England
www.lionhudson.com
UK ISBN 978 0 7459 4866 9
US ISBN 978 0 8254 7837 6

First edition 2005
3 5 7 9 10 8 6 4 2

A catalogue record for this book is available
from the British Library

Typeset in 20/24 Baskerville MT Schlbk
Printed and bound in China

Distributed by:
UK: Marston Book Services Ltd, PO Box 269
Abingdon, Oxon OX14 4YN
USA: Trafalgar Square Publishing, 814 N
Franklin Street, Chicago, IL 60610
USA Christian Market: Kregel Publications,
PO Box 2607, Grand Rapids, MI 49501

BIBLE STORY TIME

Daniel and the Lions

Sophie Piper ✳ Estelle Corke

LION
CHILDREN'S

Daniel was a very important man.
He helped King Darius rule his
empire.

He worked hard, and he was very
good at his job.

'I think I shall put Daniel in charge
of the empire,' said Darius.

The other people who worked for Darius were very cross.

'Why is Daniel getting a better job?' they muttered. 'How we wish he would make a big mistake! Then we could get rid of him.'

'You know,' said one, 'I've got an idea. Listen to my secret plan.'
They huddled close together and whispered.

Then they went to King Darius.

'Your Majesty,' they said. 'May you live for ever.

'You are great. You are wonderful. You are like a god.'

'Thank you very much,' said Darius.

'We want you to make a law,' said the men. 'No one may pray to anyone except to you. If anyone disobeys, they will be thrown into a den of lions.'

'What a splendid idea,' said Darius. 'It will be one of my great laws that cannot be changed.'

Daniel always prayed to God.
  In the morning, he prayed to God.
  In the middle of the day, he prayed to God.
  At the end of the day, he said this prayer:

'When I lie down, I sleep in peace.
Dear God, you always keep me safe.'

Daniel was not alone. The people he worked with were watching.

The next day, they went to see King Darius.

'Your Majesty,' they said. 'May you live for ever.

'Do you remember the law you made?'

'I do,' said Darius. 'It's a very strict law: no ifs, no buts, no changes.'

'Indeed it is,' said the men. 'If anyone breaks it, you will throw them into a den of lions.'

'I will,' said Darius. Then, for a bit of fun, he roared. 'Hooraaaaaah!'

'Your Majesty,' said the men.

'Daniel has broken the law. He keeps on saying prayers to his God.'

Darius stopped making roaring noises. He looked very sad. 'I don't want Daniel eaten,' he said. 'He's a very good worker. He's not included in the law.'

'Oh, but Your Majesty,' said the men. 'You CANNOT change the law.'

Darius frowned. 'Let me think,' he said. 'I'm going to find a reason why he shouldn't be included.'

He was thinking as the sun rose high in the sky. One of the men popped in to see him.

'Daniel's saying his midday prayers,' said the man.

'Go away, I'm still thinking,' said Darius.

He was thinking as the sun sank low. The same man popped back.

'Daniel's saying his evening prayers,' he said.

'Bother,' said Darius. 'It's the den for Daniel.'

Soldiers went to fetch Daniel and threw him to the lions.

Darius came to see him. 'It's all a bit of a mistake,' he called to Daniel. 'I hope your God will keep you safe.'

'Excuse me, Your Majesty,' said a soldier. 'Please move along. I'm going to block the opening to the den.

'We don't want anyone to let Daniel out, do we?'

Darius did not sleep that night.

'Oh dear, oh dear, oh dear,' he muttered. He paced up and down.

'Do you want a meal?' asked a servant. 'Or some wine?'

'No thank you,' said the king.

'Shall I play some music for you?' asked another servant.

'Stop trying to cheer me up,' said Darius. 'It just makes me more cross.'

Down in the pit, Daniel was sitting among the shadows. He couldn't see anything very clearly, but he felt sure someone was there with him. Whoever it was seemed to have a special power over the lions.

First they yawned huge, scary yawns. Then they gave little growls and fell asleep.

As soon as it was light, the king hurried to the pit.

'Daniel?' he called. 'Did your God save you?'

'May Your Majesty live for ever!' replied Daniel. 'God sent an angel to save me from the lions.'

'Hoorah!' cried Darius. This time, he didn't roar.

He helped pull Daniel to safety. 'Fetch the men who tried to kill Daniel,' he said to the soldiers. 'Put them in the pit instead.'

Then King Darius sent a message
to everyone in his empire.
 'There is no god like Daniel's God.
 'Daniel's God is strong and works
miracles to save people.
 'Everyone must respect Daniel's
God.'

Daniel went back to his old job, and he did it very, very well.